VICTORIAN LIFE

A VICTORIAN SUNDAY

SIMON AND LUCY FAULKNER

Wayland

VICTORIAN LIFE

A VICTORIAN CHRISTMAS

A VICTORIAN FACTORY

A VICTORIAN HOLIDAY

A VICTORIAN SCHOOL

A VICTORIAN STREET

A VICTORIAN SUNDAY

VICTORIAN CLOTHES

VICTORIAN TRANSPORT

HOW WE LEARN ABOUT THE VICTORIANS

Queen Victoria reigned from 1837 to 1901, a time when Britain went through enormous social and industrial changes. We can learn about Victorians in various ways. We can still see many of their buildings standing today, we can look at their documents, maps and artefacts – many of which can be found in museums. Photography, invented during Victoria's reign, gives us a good picture of life in Victorian Britain. In this book you will see what Victorian life was like through some of this historical evidence.

This edition published in 1994
by Wayland (Publishers) Ltd

First published in 1993 by Wayland (Publishers) Ltd,
61 Western Road, Hove, East Sussex BN3 1JD, England

© Copyright 1993 Wayland (Publishers) Ltd

British Library Cataloguing in Publication Data
Faulkner, Simon
  Victorian Sunday. - (Victorian Life Series)
  I. Title II. Faulkner, Lucy III. Series
  941.081

HARDBACK ISBN 0-7502-0691-8
PAPERBACK ISBN 0-7502-1369-8

Printed and bound in Great Britain by B.P.C
Paulton Books

Series design: Pardoe Blacker Ltd
Editor: Sarah Doughty

Cover picture: A mother reading a Sunday book to her children.

Picture acknowledgements
British Library Reproductions 15 (bottom), 26 (top); Mary Evans 22, 24, 26 (bottom); Billie Love Historical Collection *cover*, 5, 6, 10, 11, 12, 14, 18 (both), 20, 21 (bottom), 25, 27; Mansell Collection 7, 17; National Trust Photographic Library 9; Peter Newark's Historical Pictures 8, 16, 19; Victoria and Albert Museum 23 (top); Wayland Picture Library 21 (top); Zefa 13 (bottom). The artwork on pages 7 and 9 is by Annabel Spenceley.

Thanks to Norfolk Museums Service for supplying items from their museums on pages 4, 13 (top), 15 (top), 23 (bottom).

All commissioned photography by GGS Photo Graphics.

CONTENTS

SUNDAY
IS SPECIAL

No jokes, no games, and everyone on their best behaviour: was this the Victorian Sunday? In Victorian Britain, most people were Christians and felt that Sunday should be special, a day of rest given by God. Everyday clothes and activities were not good enough for Sunday. Anybody who forgot this would find themselves frowned upon.

DAY OF REST

Victorians had a strong sense of duty. God had given each person a place in life and tasks to do. Even having a day of rest did not mean doing whatever you felt like. The day was spent in ways which showed respect and gratitude to God. Normal work and play were unsuitable. Shops were shut, although you could buy bread on Sunday morning and milk before 9 am or after 4 pm. Surprisingly, letters were delivered on Sunday.

People were expected to do their 'Sunday duty' and go to church or chapel at least once. Those who worked as servants would go to church but then might have half the day to themselves.

A Victorian calendar.

FAMILY DAY

Sunday was a family day. For many working people, Sunday was their only day off. It was the one day when the whole family could be together.

In rich households there would be a servant called a nurse who looked after the children. For most of the week the children would see very little of their parents. But on a Sunday, dressed in their best clothes and on their best behaviour, children would share the grown-ups' meals and spend time with their parents and the other adults of the family. This photograph shows how three generations of a family would have dressed on a Sunday.

A family at home in 1888.

SUNDAY BEST

Do you enjoy wearing your best clothes? Victorian children probably had less choice about their clothes than you do. They were put into clothes thought suitable for their age and sex, almost like a uniform. Nearly every Victorian child had one set of clothes they would keep for Sunday best.

SUNDAY FINERY

Victorian children's best clothes were not very comfortable. They were often easily spoilt. If this boy on the right climbed a tree his white suit would be ruined, and if his sister ran in the garden she might tear a frill. Although they might feel rather grand in their finery, putting on Sunday clothes meant putting on Sunday manners. Sometimes in order to take care of Sunday clothes, children changed up to three times a day, only putting on their best to go out.

Children in early Victorian fashions.

UNDERGARMENTS

A girl in the 1800s wore two pairs of combinations – one made of wool and the other of cotton. Combinations were one-piece garments – made up of a vest and pants which covered down to the knees. A pair of stays was worn on the upper part of the body, a petticoat, and on top of all this, a dress.

Boys wore combinations as undergarments too. Over the combinations they wore shirts and suits. Sailor suits were popular for boys. Both boys and girls wore hats on Sundays.

WASHING

It was important to have best clothes clean, dry and ironed ready for Sunday. Monday was the usual day for washing. If the family was poor and had few clothes, washing had to be done on Sunday. It was the only chance to wash a man's working suit while he wore his best suit. If he did not have one, he stayed in bed!

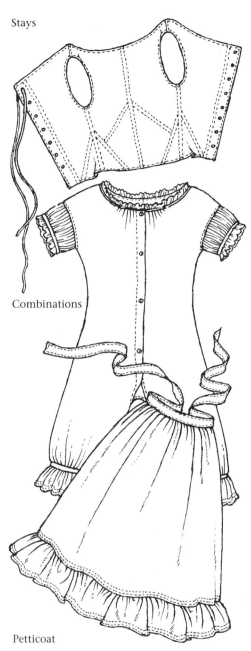

Stays

Combinations

Petticoat

The undergarments worn by Victorian girls.

Sunday morning in a working-class home, London 1875.

SUNDAY MEALS

If you travelled back in time to a Victorian household, you might be surprised by the food. In a poor family, it would seem very dull, and you might complain that there was not enough to eat. If you were in a rich family, you might be amazed at the amount of food eaten. Sunday meals were usually bigger and better than weekday meals. The difference was more important for poorer people, whose Sunday meals would bring the only treats they had.

Breakfast, 1888.

BREAKFAST

In a poor family, breakfast was usually bread with jam or lard, and tea. Anything extra, such as an egg, would be for the father on Sunday. In rich families, dinner was late and breakfast could be a large meal with hot dishes of eggs, kidneys, bacon, sausages and chops. Then there might be cold ham, tongue and pies, plus muffins, toast, tea and coffee. Not everybody had the appetite for such a large meal. This family is satisfied with eggs, bread and coffee.

MEAT FOR DINNER

Working people had Sunday dinner in the middle of the day. It might be the only day of the week they had meat, even if it was only small pieces in their 'pudding'. The pudding, like a dumpling, was wrapped in a cloth and boiled in the pot with vegetables. If the family could afford a piece of meat to roast, it could be hung before the fire, or cooked on a spit with a tray to catch the dripping.

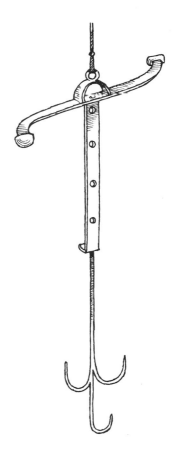

A spit for cooking meat.

KITCHEN RANGE

Better-off families had a kitchen range, similar to the one shown here. A kitchen range would have several ovens which could be used for roasting and baking. When people could afford to, it was normal to eat several dishes for each course. On a kitchen range, several types of meat could be cooked at the same time, so roast meat could be served at the same time as boiled meat.

This is the Sunday dinner that was served in a successful builder's house in Oxfordshire in the 1880s. Relatives came for the day, so there were four adults and four children to eat the meal, and one servant to help with the cooking.

> Roast leg of lamb
> Two boiled fowls, garnished with slices of ham
> Jellies and cheesecakes

AFTERNOON TEA

Many households, rich and poor, had a cake specially baked for Sunday. In poor families this would appear at the last meal of the day, along with bread and butter. For the better off, there would also be supper or dinner later, so the bread and butter was cut thinly, and not so much was eaten. In later Victorian times when people were not so strict about travelling, Sunday tea-time became a good time to go visiting friends and relatives.

Tea in the garden.

SERVANTS

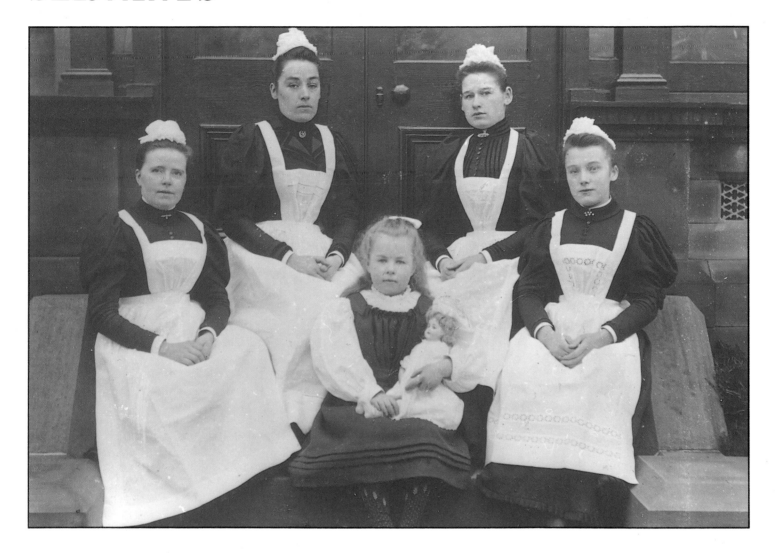

Servants with the daughter of the house, 1898.

Everybody who could afford to would employ servants to work for them. Sometimes a household would have just one servant, but in large houses there could be dozens. With many servants to do the work, Victorian meals were elaborate and often took hours to prepare. Sometimes the servants were given less work on Sunday. If the main meal was at 1.30 pm instead of in the evening, there could be a cold supper, leaving the servants free all afternoon.

CHURCH
AND CHAPEL

Religion played a part in almost every Victorian child's life. Most families would go to church or chapel at least once on a Sunday. Children were expected to behave like adults in church. Imagine sitting on a hard seat for over an hour without fidgeting or whispering once.

Church at Brading, Isle of Wight.

ATTENDING CHURCH OR CHAPEL

Most Christians in England and Wales belonged to the Church of England and went to their parish church. Others chose the new chapels with their lively preaching and simpler services. There were also Catholics in most areas.

Not everybody went to church or chapel each week. One Sunday in 1851, everybody in the country who attended church or chapel was counted. Just over 40 people in every hundred went to a service on that day. If you lived in a town perhaps no one noticed if you missed church. In villages, children were sometimes punished at school on Monday for missing church on Sunday.

INSIDE A CHURCH

In the Church of England the best pews were bought or rented. Wealthy people made themselves comfortable in pews with cushions. Poor people often felt less welcome. Those who could not afford to pay for seats stayed at the back, sometimes standing. Some people turned to the new Methodist or Baptist chapels because they felt that God was more interested in whether they were good than whether they were rich.

The interior of a church.

A church in the Scottish highlands.

THE CHURCH IN SCOTLAND

In Scotland, the Episcopal Church had very similar services to those of the Church of England. But the Episcopal Church was not the main Church of Scotland. The Church of Scotland was, and still is, Presbyterian. Not everybody attended these churches – some attended the Roman Catholic Church, while others attended the new chapels or the Free Church which was started up in 1843.

Children singing in church.

THE CHURCH SERVICE

Hymns were sung in church but, between the hymns, services in England followed the Prayer Book closely. In the Presbyterian Church in Scotland, they did not follow liturgy or the Prayer Book.

Nonconformist chapel services had more variety, with visiting preachers. Sometimes people told the story of how they changed from a sinful life and started to believe in Jesus. Sermons were preached in both church and chapel. The preachers tried to stir up people's feelings, making them ashamed of wrongdoing, grateful for God's gifts, or afraid of Hell if they died as sinners.

CITY MISSIONS

Both the Church of England and the Nonconformist churches were worried that there were more and more people in Britain who did not believe in God or know about Jesus. Perhaps they saw children in crowded parts of big cities whose parents never attended church, were often drunk and unable to teach their children right from wrong. City Missions were set up and preachers went to the poorest areas to persuade people to come to special services.

Poster for a City Mission meeting.

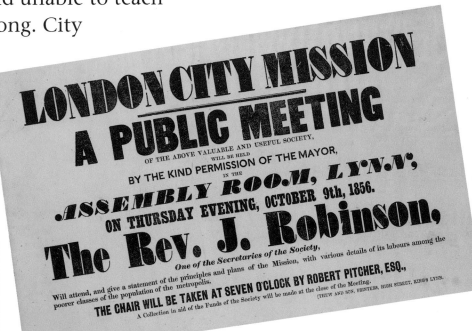

A CATECHISM,

THAT IS TO SAY,

AN INSTRUCTION TO BE LEARNED OF EVERY PERSON, BEFORE HE BE BROUGHT TO BE CONFIRMED BY THE BISHOP.

Question.
WHAT is your Name?

Answer.
N. or M.

Question.
Who gave you this Name?

Answer.
My Godfathers and Godmothers in my Baptism; wherein I was made a member of Christ, the Child of God, and an inheritor of the kingdom of heaven.

Question.
What did your Godfathers and Godmothers then for you?

Answer.
They did promise and vow three things in my name. First, that I should renounce the devil and all his works, the pomps and vanity of this wicked world, and all the sinful lusts of the flesh. Secondly, that I should believe all the Articles of the Christian Faith. And thirdly, that I should keep God's holy will and commandments, and walk in the same all the days of my life.

Question.
Dost thou not think that thou art bound to believe, and to do, as they have promised for thee?

Answer.
Yes verily; and by God's help so I will. And I heartily thank our heavenly Father, that He hath called

The first page from the catechism.

THE CATECHISM

Children were expected to learn to understand what it meant to be a Christian. To help them they were taught the catechism, which you can find in the Book of Common Prayer. It is a set of questions and answers to be learned by heart. As well as helping their children to learn the catechism, some parents made them learn parts of the Bible or prayers from the week's service.

SUNDAY SCHOOL

Would you like to go to school on Sunday? For some Victorian children this was their only chance to learn to read and write. It was also a chance to mix with other children on a day when most games were forbidden. If you went every week you might get a prize, and there was also the Sunday School treat to look forward to.

TEACHING IN THE SUNDAY SCHOOL

Children were sent to Sunday School even if their parents did not usually go to church. In the early part of Victoria's reign there were few non-fee paying schools for children. The churches and chapels found that to teach children to read the Bible they first had to teach them to read. The younger children would take slates to write on. Parents found it useful to send their children out, giving them an hour's peace at home. There were morning and afternoon Sunday Schools, so if children went to church in the morning, they would go to Sunday School in the afternoon.

Children off to Sunday School.

SUNDAY SCHOOL LESSONS

The Sunday School teacher, in 1885.

In church Sunday Schools the job of teacher was often taken on by the clergyman's wife or daughter. Teachers at chapel Sunday Schools were chosen because they were true Christians, but they were often poorly educated. Bright pupils sometimes knew more than their teachers. All that most teachers had to help them were copies of the Bible or the catechism. The children were divided into groups of the same age. Some groups were led by older pupils, called monitors, or by assistant teachers.

SUNDAY SCHOOL REWARDS

Children who had been to school all week might have preferred not to go to Sunday School. To encourage them to go, Sunday Schools gave prizes for attendance and good behaviour. The best children would be given certificates like this one and, often, a book as a reward. There would also be a treat or an outing once a year.

Just as in ordinary schools at that time, the teacher would keep a cane handy to punish children who did not pay attention or were cheeky.

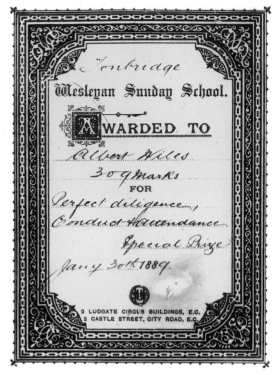

An attendance certificate.

HYMN SINGING

Singing hymns made a change from Bible study. Many hymns for children were written at this time. For example:

Do no sinful action,
Speak no angry word;
Ye belong to Jesus,
Children of the Lord.

Christ is kind and gentle,
Christ is pure and true,
And His little children
Must be holy too.

Singing in Sunday School in 1896.

SUNDAY MAGAZINES

Magazines like this one were written to encourage children to care about people less fortunate than themselves. In the magazine, they would read about children in slums who were not taught about Jesus. There were also stories about children whose parents were unable to care for them because of drinking alcohol. Some Victorian Christians encouraged children to make a solemn promise that they would never drink alcohol.

From 1847 they called the organization against alcohol the 'Band of Hope'. It started in Leeds, and gradually gained branches all over the country.

Our Own Magazine,
1894.

TREATS AND OUTINGS

How many times do you go on an outing each year? Victorian treats may sound tame compared with the theme parks and fairgrounds of today, but Victorian children enjoyed these special occasions. Once a year, every Sunday School celebrated the day it was founded. Every church and chapel also had a Sunday School treat. Lucky children were taken on a trip as well as being given an especially good tea.

THE PARADE

Celebrating the founding of a Sunday School in 1871.

This Sunday School is celebrating the day it was founded. The day began with a parade of handsome banners. The children would stop and sing carefully-practised hymns. Some children might recite poems, on their own or in pairs, before tea. Children who had recited were sometimes rewarded with an orange.

SUNDAY SCHOOL TREAT

Part of the excitement of the Sunday School treat was getting to it. In country areas farm horses and wagons were often used. When several Sunday Schools joined together there would be a long and merry procession of wagons laden with children on benches. Children from one Hampshire village used to be taken to the seaside behind a steam traction engine. Unfortunately the sparks burnt holes in their clothes!

A steam traction engine.

CANAL BOAT TRIP

These children from a church Sunday School were taken on a canal boat. When tea was unpacked, the children had more bread, butter and cake than most of them were used to.

Children on a canal boat.

After tea there were games. Perhaps there would be 'scrambling' after sweets and nuts thrown by a teacher. Then the children might stand in a circle for traditional round games like Jenny-sits-a-weeping, or play chasing games like tag.

SUNDAY PASTIMES

For Victorians, Sunday was a holiday from school and work but it was also a holy day. Children were brought up to be quiet and serious on Sunday. Most of their usual pastimes were forbidden. There were few toys or games, almost no books, no sports, travel or entertainment. This meant there was very little to do once you had been to church and Sunday School. So how did Victorian families pass the long slow hours of Sunday?

SATURDAY EVENING

Here is a working man's family on Saturday night. Before bedtime, the boys' bricks, the little girl's doll and mother's mending will all be put away until Monday. The next evening, Sunday, they will gather round the fire again. The big Bible will be down from the shelf and perhaps another book kept specially for Sunday. The children amuse themselves looking at the pictures.

A working class family at home, 1861.

On Sunday the children will talk quietly so as not to disturb father reading his Sunday newspaper. Perhaps before bedtime father puts aside his paper and reads aloud from the Bible. Then the children go to bed and say their prayers, pleased that the long day is over.

SUNDAY TOYS

Luckily, there were some toys which were allowed because they taught children stories from the Bible. A Noah's Ark, with Noah, his family and all the pairs of animals, as shown to the right, was a favourite. There were also jigsaws and brick puzzles which fitted together to show scenes from the life of Jesus. This one shows Jesus raising a child from the dead.

Noah's Ark

Building blocks with a religious picture.

AFTERNOON WALK

In the afternoon many families went for a walk.
These Londoners are taking their walk in Hyde
Park. The boys are being allowed to sail model
yachts. Perhaps some of the passers-by think it
is an unsuitable thing to do on Sunday. But
even if you had to walk along on your best
behaviour it was better than staying indoors
with next to nothing to do. You could see your
friends and neighbours and show off your best
clothes. What Victorian children dreaded above
all was a *wet* Sunday.

A walk in the park.

A family picnic.

A PICNIC

One of the things a family could do together on
Sunday was have a picnic. They would pack
buns and sandwiches into a basket and walk to
a favourite place. People tried not to travel by
carriage or train on Sunday unless the journey
was very important. But most Victorians lived
quite close to their relations, and it was easy to
meet them for a picnic tea.

Some families were stricter than others and
looked on disapprovingly while others enjoyed
themselves. As Victoria's reign went on, people
became a little less strict about Sunday. Then it
became more usual to go visiting and invite
people for meals on Sundays.

READING BOOKS

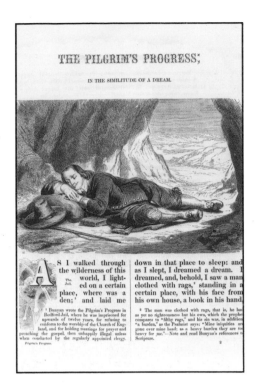

The first page from *The Pilgrim's Progress*.

Children were encouraged to read books which taught them about their religion. *The Pilgrim's Progress* was found in many homes, but it was written by John Bunyan in the seventeenth century and is difficult to read. The hero is called Christian and his adventures show what it is like trying to be a Christian. There were books written specially for children to read on Sundays. Mrs Sherwood copied John Bunyan and wrote *The Infant's Progress*. She also wrote *The Fairchild Family*, a very popular set of stories to show how three children learned to be good.

MUSIC

Many better-off families enjoyed music. There were no radios or recordings in Victorian times, so the family had to make its own music. Only religious music was allowed on Sundays. The family would gather round the piano, taking turns to choose favourite hymns to sing.

Family music.

GOOD-NIGHT PRAYERS

Victorian parents made sure their children said their prayers before they went to sleep. Every night a child would say the Lord's Prayer, beginning 'Our Father', and would ask God to bless all the family. Another prayer often used by children at this time was:

Good-night prayers.

Gentle Jesus meek and mild,
Look upon this little child.
Pity my simplicity;
Suffer me to come to thee.

Many children learnt this by heart without understanding it. A simpler bedtime prayer was:

Now I lay me down to
    sleep,
I pray the Lord my soul to
    keep;
And if I die before I wake,
I pray the Lord my soul to
    take.

TIME LINE

EARLY 1800s

1803 Sunday School Union formed to help Sunday Schools in London and elsewhere and to provide books.

1818 Mrs Sherwood's *The Fairchild Family* published (Part One).

1819 Queen Victoria born.

1829 Catholic Emancipation Act passed, which let Catholics become Members of Parliament.

1830s

1831 Lord's Day Observance Society founded to help keep Sunday a day for rest and worship.

1833 Oxford Movement in Church of England begins. Its aim was to restore the Catholic tradition and ritual of the Church.

1837 Queen Victoria's reign begins.

1840s

1846 Evangelical Alliance formed. This was an international group to support Christians who thought that belief in the Bible was more important than ritual.

The boys' sailor suit was made popular by the young Prince of Wales.

1847 The 'Band of Hope' started.

1850s

1851 A census shows 40 per cent of people in Britain attend church or chapel.

Queen Victoria's purchase of Balmoral in Scotland makes wearing tartan fashionable.

1854 Holman Hunt painted *The Light of the World*, a picture of Jesus which became very popular.

1860s

1859-65 Mrs Beeton's Cookery Book published and printed three times.

1861 Dr Barnardo's East End Mission to help homeless boys in London.

1866 *Alice in Wonderland* by Lewis Carroll published.

1870s

1871 Bank Holidays introduced.

1874 Public Worship Regulation Act to make sure that clergymen of the Church of England did not bring Catholic customs into their services.

1878 William Booth founds the Salvation Army.

1880s

1883 Foundation of the Boy's Brigade.

1886 *Little Lord Fauntleroy* published, making velvet suits popular for boys.

1890s

1896 Museums and art galleries allowed to open on Sundays.

1900s

1901 Queen Victoria dies.

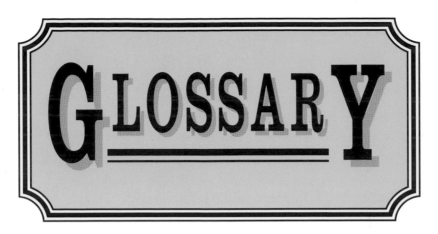
GLOSSARY

Attendance Being present at an event.

Catholic Christians who follow the leadership of the Pope.

Clergyman A man whose job it is to hold services in the Church of England and to look after the people of the parish.

Combinations Underwear made up of vest and pants together, often made of cotton or woollen material.

Duty A task, or way of behaving suitable to who you are.

Episcopal A Church governed by bishops.

Fowls Chickens.

Garnished Decorated.

Lard Pig's fat. Cottage housewives would make a year's supply when they killed their pig.

Liturgy The form of service laid down by the church.

Missions Groups of Christians working to persuade others to become Christian.

Muffins Plain buns made with yeast.

Nonconformists Methodists, Baptists and other Christians who broke away from the Church of England.

Parish Division of the country which has its own church.

Protestant The Christians who, since the sixteenth century, refused to accept the leadership of the Pope.

Presbyterian Protestant Church with lay elders (senior members who are not clergymen).

Range A coal-burning stove, often with several ovens and a water boiler.

Recite To say out loud something which has been learned by heart.

Slates Thin pieces of stone slate, usually mounted in a frame, used by schoolchildren to write on.

Slums Overcrowded houses, often without drains or water supply.

Stays A firm padded vest, laced up the front, worn by girls.

BOOKS TO READ

Chamberlin, E. *Everyday Life in the Nineteenth Century* (Macdonald Educational, 1983)

Conner, E. A. *A Child in Victorian London* (Wayland, 1986)

Evans, D. *How We Used To Live – Victorians Early and Late* (A & C Black, 1989)

Harper, R. *Finding Out About Victorian Childhood* (Batsford, 1986)

Ross, S. *Spotlight on the Victorians* (Wayland, 1988)

Thompson, F. To Church on Sunday (Chapter XIV) in *Lark Rise to Candleford* (1939); also Chapter XXI, Over To Candleford

Triggs, T. *Victorian Britain* (Wayland, 1990)

PLACES TO VISIT

The following museums have displays and exhibitions to do with social history.

ENGLAND

Avon: Blaise Castle House, Henby, Bristol, BS10 7QS. Tel. 0272 506789

Cheshire: Quarry Bank Mill, Styal, SK9 4LA. Tel. 0625 527468

County Durham: North of England Open Air Museum, Beamish, DH9 ORG. Tel. 0207 231811

Humberside:Wilberforce House, 25 High Street, Hull, HU1 3EP. Tel. 0482 593902

Lancashire: Museum of Childhood, Lancaster, LA1 1YS. Tel. 0524 32808

London: Victoria and Albert Museum, South Kensington, SW7 2RL. Tel. 071 938 8500

Museum of Childhood, Cambridge Heath Road, London E2 9PA. Tel. 081 980 2415

Merseyside: Toy Museum, 42 Bridge Street Row, Chester, CH1 1RS. Tel. 0244 346297

Norfolk: Gressenhall Rural Life Museum, Dereham, NR20 4DR. Tel. 0362 860563

Shropshire: Iron Bridge Gorge Museum, Blists Hill Site, Telford, TS8 7AW. Tel. 0952 433522

Warwickshire: St. John's House Museum, Warwick, CV34 4NF. Tel. 0926 412034

Yorkshire: York Castle Museum, York, YO1 1RY. Tel: 0904 653611

SCOTLAND

Angus: Angus Folk Museum, Glamis, Forfar, DD8 1RT. Tel. 037 84288

WALES

Cardiff: Welsh Folk Museum, St. Fagans, CF5 6XB. Tel. 0222 569441

INDEX

BRITISH HISTORY

Early Britain

500,000 BC–AD 1154

KINGFISHER

 KINGFISHER

First published in 1992 by Kingfisher
This revised, reformatted and updated
edition published in 2007 by Kingfisher
an imprint of Macmillan Children's Books
20 New Wharf Road, London N1 9RR
Associated companies around the world
www.panmacmillan.com

Consultants: Dr Paul Bahn, David Haycock

ISBN 978 0 7534 1475 0

This edition copyright © Macmillan Publishers International Ltd 2007

Material in this edition previously published by Kingfisher in the
Children's Illustrated Encyclopedia of British History in 1992

3 5 7 9 8 6 4 2
2SPL/0416/UTD/WKT/115MA

A CIP catalogue record for this book is available from the British Library.

Printed in China

CONTENTS

EARLY BRITAIN

(c. 500,000 BC – AD 440)

THE EARLY STORY OF BRITAIN starts some half a million years ago in prehistory (the vast period of time before written records). The earliest people hunted animals and gathered food from what was around them. These hunters and gatherers began to build camps, some of which have been discovered. From the stone tools and other remains found at these sites we can learn what life was like before recorded history. Later hunters discovered how to make and use metals such as bronze and copper, and also started to keep sheep and cattle – the first farmers. They built primitive villages and dug huge ditches to make hill forts. At about the time the Egyptians were building the Great Pyramid of Giza, the earliest Britons started to build Stonehenge (*below*) – one of the most remarkable prehistoric stone structures in the world. Britain was still a fairly primitive land compared with Egypt and other major civilizations. By about 500 BC, however, Celtic tribes had settled in Britain and were making iron weapons and utensils, using wheeled carts and chariots and building impressive hill-forts such as Maiden Castle in Dorset.

Stonehenge may have been laid out to mark the position of the midsummer sunrise.

Early Britain

THE EARLIEST HISTORY OF BRITAIN starts in the period known as prehistory, before writing was invented. In Britain, the first written records were introduced by the Romans, so anything that happened in Britain before the Roman Conquest in 55 BC is prehistory.

THE OLD STONE AGE

Archaeologists, people who dig up and examine the remains of prehistory and later periods of history, have discovered two open-air camps near Clacton-on-Sea in Essex and Boxgrove in Sussex. Both sites contain human and animal bones and masses of stone tools. The earliest people lived on this land as long ago as 500,000 years in what is called the Old Stone Age.

In these prehistoric times, there were four great Ice Ages when much of the land was covered by thick ice sheets. In the warmer spells the ice retreated and Old Stone Age people roamed over tundra. Britain was joined to France by open grasslands over what is now the English Channel. People sheltered in caves, and in tents made from animal skin, and they could make fires – which helped them to survive the harsh conditions.

 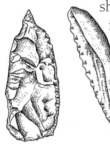

Above: **A flint axe from the Old Stone Age, about a quarter of its real size. Early inhabitants also made flint-tipped spears.**

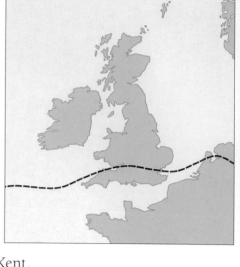

Right: **In the Ice Age Britain was covered by ice north of the Thames estuary (*see dotted line on map*). The land was also joined to Europe across the Channel (*see area shaded in green*).**

HUNTER-GATHERERS

At a place called Swanscombe, in Kent, archaeologists have discovered the remains of a young woman who lived almost 200,000 years ago. She was one of the prehistoric people known as hunter-gatherers. They used sharp stone tools and hand-axes to hunt and fish, but they did not yet domesticate, or tame, animals such as the reindeer and horses which surrounded them. They gathered and ate wild berries, nuts, fruit and roots but did not cultivate, or grow anything. Their stone flake tools and axes have been discovered by archaeologists in many parts of Britain and can been seen today in museums around the country.

The Old Stone Age people lived in small family groups of a dozen or so, and used flint tools to scrape reindeer, mammoth and other animal skins and to bore holes into them. They sewed these hides into clothes using animal tissue threaded on bone needles.

TIME CHART
Note: Dates are approximate

● **500,000 to 4500 BC** Old Stone Age (also called Palaeolithic) period

● **500,000 to 300,000 BC** Early people using flint tools near Clacton-on-Sea

● **500,000 BC** Boxgrove open-air camp in Sussex

● **125,000 BC** Last period of glaciation (ice cover) begins

● **40,000 BC** Early people in caves at Creswell Crags, Derbyshire

A NOTE ABOUT DATES
The letters **BC** indicate the years **B**efore **C**hrist was born; these are placed after the year, and are numbered backwards, so 55 BC (the first Roman invasion), then 54 BC (the second Roman invasion). The letters **AD** indicate the years after Christ was born (**A**nno **D**omini is Latin for Year of Our Lord.) The letters are placed before the year and are numbered forwards, so AD 410 (when the Romans left Britain) is followed by AD 411.

Left: **Well over 200,000 years ago, Britain's first settlers could make hand-axes using blocks of stones, usually flint.**

Left: **Making fires and sewing animal hides were key activities for early Britons.**

Right. **The first cave paintings and carvings, such as this bison carved in bone, were made in prehistoric times.**

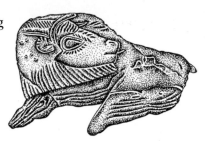

It was the switch to keeping animals and sowing crops, as well as still hunting and fishing for food, that marked the New Stone Age period in Britain.

With farming and settlement came other skills, such as using deer antlers to break the soil for sowing, and making pottery bowls. Some people became flint-miners, using sharp and polished stone axes. The flint mines at Grimes Graves in Norfolk show they could sink shafts over ten metres deep. People also now buried their dead in long burial mounds called barrows which were like chambers. A New Stone Age camp at Windmill Hill in Wiltshire has a group of round barrows. Another site, at Skara Brae in the Orkneys, is claimed to be the oldest village. In the 1920s a storm washed away the sand-hills that had kept it hidden and protected for 5,000 years.

THE NEW STONE AGE

As the ice melted it released more water into the sea until, around 6000 BC, the last land bridge disappeared and Britain was cut off from Europe by the English Channel. But traders and settlers still came to Britain, on boats and rafts. From about 4500 BC the New Stone Age began as people started farming rather more than hunting and gathering for food. Settlers and traders brought seed corn, sheep and cattle with them and, using sharp axeheads fitted onto wooden handles, they cleared the woods around them so their animals could graze and so they could sow crops of wheat and barley. They were the first farmers.

Below: **At Skara Brae in the Orkneys, north of Scotland, you can visit New Stone Age houses built around 3100 BC. They are well preserved, with cupboards and beds** made from slabs of local Orkney stone. The people here wore beads of teeth and bone, made peat fires and kept sheep. The soil was too windswept to grow crops.

- ● **3200 BC** Stonehenge, Wiltshire, begun

- ● **3100 BC** Stone Age village at Skara Brae, Orkney

- ● **2600 BC** Silbury Hill, a huge barrow in Wiltshire, built

- ● **2500 BC** First known British pottery at Windmill Hill, Wiltshire

- ● **2000 BC** First known weaving

- ● **1900 BC** Beaker Folk arrive in Britain, with bronze tools

- ● **1800 BC** Bronze Age begins in Britain

- ● **800 BC** First Celts invade

- ● **700 BC** Iron Age begins in Britain

- ● **350 BC** Celts settle in Ireland

- ● **200 BC** Celts settle in Taymouth and Moray Firth

Above: **Stonehenge was built in three stages, beginning about 3200 BC and ending about 1300 BC. Huge standing stones such as these are called megaliths (from the Greek *mega-*, large, and *lith*, stone), and are scattered throughout northern Europe. They may have been used to observe the sun, moon and stars, as well as to record the seasons.**

Below: **Around 4,000 years ago the first farming villages appeared, made of wood and thatched straw. The people grew barley and wheat and learned to spin and weave wool. They also made simple pots from clay.**

THE BRONZE AGE

From around 1800 BC, people began to make metal tools and knife-daggers of bronze, by mixing copper with tin over very hot fires. Britain had plenty of tin, copper and even gold. Britain first became known to the classical world of Greece and Rome as the Cassiterides, the Islands of Tin. The island inhabitants continued the New Stone Age way of life, clearing woods to make open land for growing crops and erecting more dwellings.

STONEHENGE AND AVEBURY

These early settlers also built the most spectacular Bronze Age site in Europe, at Stonehenge, on Salisbury Plain in Wiltshire. It includes a ring of 80 massive rocks that were brought from the Prescelly Mountains in southern Wales, a journey of about 390 kilometres. The huge sandstone blocks in the centre were dragged from Avebury, 30 kilometres away. Avebury itself has an even larger henge, or stone circle. Though less well preserved, it is even older than Stonehenge. Passing through Avebury is the Ridgeway, an ancient road just over 150 kilometres long, that can still be travelled.

THE CELTS AND THE IRON AGE

Around 700 BC, the first iron-using tribes, the Celts, arrived from Europe. They knew how to make much stronger iron weapons, nails and tools such as axes and saws. They used sturdy war chariots and armour, and made bronze, rather than flint, sickles for reaping corn, They also made the first bronze musical horns, and gold cups and jewellery. By about 500 BC the first wheeled carts were in use on Britain's ancient routes.

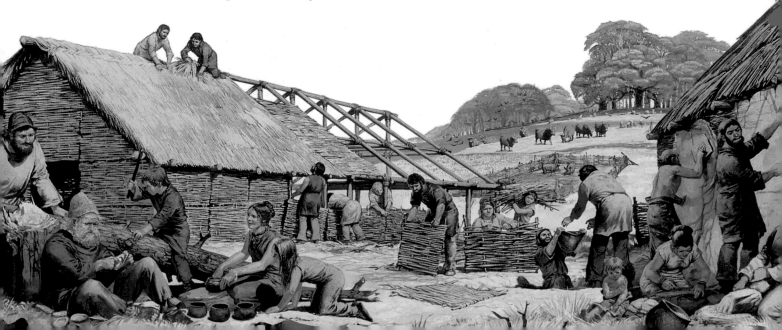

Right: **Celtic families lived with their chickens and dogs in huts grouped within the safe ramparts of a hill-fort. The frame of the hut was made of wooden posts, the walls of wattle and daub, and the roof of thatch or straw. A big iron cauldron hung from a crossbeam.**

Walls of carefully woven branches plastered over with clay. This is known as wattle and daub and can still be seen on old houses today.

The Celtic tribes who settled in Britain, and their descendants, are called Britons. Their language is still spoken today, because Welsh, Gaelic, Irish and Cornish are directly related to Celtic. For example, the Celtic word for river is *avon*. The Celts left no written records themselves, but the Romans wrote about them, and their first accounts of these islands tell of Celtic life in Britain.

These Iron Age Britons built great hill-forts, the best known of which is Maiden Castle in Dorset. They were built on high ground with commanding views of the surrounding countryside, and were made of rock and earth dug out of the ground with very deep and steep-sided slopes. Inside were enough circular thatched dwellings to make up a small town. Tribal life was dominated by the chieftains, their warriors, and by priests called druids.

Although the Celts conquered much of Europe, their power was eventually threatened by the well-organized armies of the Roman empire.

The Romans

BY 100 BC THE ROMANS had an empire that bordered all of the Mediterranean Sea, and stretched across most of Europe, North Africa and the Middle East up to the Red Sea. The Roman army's legions had conquered France, which was called Gaul, and were poised to cross the English Channel. Their knowledge of Britain came from the reports of traders. At first, invasion was not considered worthwhile because the goods the island had to offer – tin, cloth, corn, gold and slaves – could be taken from other tribes on the Continent. But army commanders, including Julius Caesar, the governor of Gaul, wanted more victories. He was troubled by Celtic revolts which had support from tribes in the south of Britain.

ROMAN INVASIONS

Julius Caesar landed on the English coast, probably at Deal, near Dover, Kent, in 55 BC. Although he had 10,000 troops and cavalry, storms damaged his ships and after fierce fighting with the Britons he had to retreat. In 54 BC, the Romans made a second invasion, moving inland and taking the hill-fort of Bigbury, near Canterbury. The British tribes were now under one chief, Cassivellaunus of the Catuvellauni tribe, whose base was north of the River Thames near modern-day St Albans. Caesar's well-organized Roman troops crossed the River Medway, then the Thames, and forced the Britons to submit to him.

But revolt in Gaul and civil war in Rome took Caesar and his army away, never to return. The Catuvellauni grew strong again under their chief Cunobelinus. For the next 100 years they controlled the southeast with their capital at Camulodunum, now Colchester, in Essex.

- **75 BC** Catuvellauni tribe (from present-day Belgium) settle at Colchester

- **55 BC** Julius Caesar invades Britain near Dover, but has to retreat

- **54 BC** Caesar raids again with five legions and reaches Essex

- *c.* **5 BC** Birth of Jesus Christ

- *c.* **AD 30** Crucifixion of Jesus

- **AD 43** Four Roman legions under Aulus Plautius invade Britain

- **AD 44** Emperor Claudius arrives in Britain and captures Camulodunum (Colchester)

- **AD 45** Vespasian (later emperor) captures Vectis (the Isle of Wight)

- **AD 47** Ostorius Scapula defeats the Iceni in East Anglia

- **AD 48** Romans begin conquest of Wales

- **AD 51** Caractacus (Caradog), King of the Silures, is captured and taken to Rome

Above: **A Roman soldier with shield, spear, short stabbing sword and light armour. In total he carried about 30 kg of equipment.**

Below: **Roman soldiers fought in groups called legions, fighting in formation with swords and spears and protecting themselves with shields.**

ROMAN RULE

In AD 43, the Emperor Claudius sent 40,000 troops under the command of Aulus Plautius, to conquer Britain. Claudius came the next year and entered Camulodunum (Colchester) in triumph. Caractacus led the British resistance for the next seven years. He was eventually handed over to the Romans by Queen Cartimandua of the Brigantes, a northern tribe, who had signed a treaty with the Romans when he fled to her for refuge. Caractacus was led through the streets of Rome bound in chains.

BOUDICCA'S REVOLT

In AD 60 Prasutagus, King of the Iceni, a Norfolk tribe, died and left his fortune jointly to his two daughters and the Roman emperor. The Romans proceeded to take over the kingdom, and Catus, the Roman treasurer, seized all of the king's dominions, ill-treated the daughters and had their mother, Queen Boudicca, publicly bound and scourged. Outraged, Boudicca led a fierce revolt. Under her leadership the Iceni burned Camulodunum (Colchester), Verulamium (St Albans) and Londinium (London) and slaughtered many Romans. The Romans rallied under their governor and defeated Boudicca, who killed herself. Organized resistance by British tribes to Rome was over.

Britain was now the furthest northwest province of the Roman empire. The Romans needed to protect the valuable British minerals such as tin, iron ore, gold and lead. Roman troops went as far as Exeter in Devon, and to the coast and valleys of Wales. In 1996 archaeologists reported that they had discovered a Roman fort on the coast of Ireland which shows the Romans might have established a foothold even further west than was previously believed. But the troops could not control what is now Scotland, where they encountered the fierce Pictish, or painted, tribes.

HADRIAN'S WALL

In AD 122 the Emperor Hadrian visited Britain – the first to do so since Claudius – and decided to establish a secure northern frontier for the Roman province. So, he ordered a wall to be built across the narrowest part of the country, from the river Tyne to the Solway Firth. Hadrian's Wall, a great work of military engineering, stretched across the country for 117 kilometres.

Above: **Boudicca, Queen of the Iceni (in modern Norfolk) in her war chariot. She headed a great revolt against the Romans but was defeated in AD 62. She took her own life.**

Below: **The Romans left over 9,000 km of straight roads in Britain, including the Fosse Way from Lincoln down into Devon. They also built the famous** Hadrian's Wall, and the not so well known Antonine Wall, made of turf and stretching 60 km from present-day Glasgow to Edinburgh.

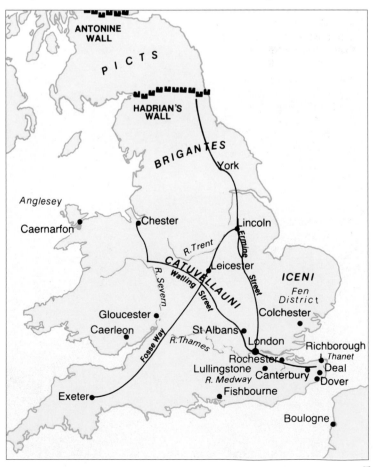

Above: **Roman roads were paved with thick slabs of stone and raised in the centre so rainwater ran into ditches at the sides. Many stretches of these roads still exist.**

Below: **The Romans enjoyed public baths and the most famous in Britain are located at Bath in Avon. Aquae Sulis, as Bath was called, fell into Saxon hands in** AD 577. **Roman baths had 1 an** exercise area (*palaestra*); **2 changing room** (*apodyterium*); **3 cool bath** (*frigidarium*); **4 warm bath** (*tepidarium*); **5 hot room** (*caldarium*); **6 underfloor heating system** (*hypocaust*).

Hadrian's Wall took seven years to complete, and long stretches of it still stand today at a height of 2 metres. The wall was made of stone about 4.5 metres high and 3 metres thick, with a ditch on the north side. A second ditch, or vallum, was later dug to the south. About every 1.5 kilometres stood a small fort called a milecastle – a barracks for between 25 and 50 men. In total, as many as 5,000 troops might have been needed to guard, supply and to look after the entire wall's defences. There were also 17 major forts added to the wall at regular distances. These were really small military towns with headquarters, barracks for the troops to sleep in, workshops for weapons and tools, a hospital and a large granary for food supplies. One fort, at Birdoswald in Cumbria, had 1,000 people.

LIFE IN ROMAN BRITAIN

From AD 70 onwards for 100 years, Britain under Roman rule was peaceful and prosperous. But what other benefits did the Romans bring? Perhaps most importantly they brought a written language, Latin, and written numbers. The history of Britain was now recorded on paper and many of the first accounts have been passed down by Roman writers. The Romans were also highly organized: they introduced a ten month calendar, and fixed hours of the day.

They also built a huge network of roads, including Fosse Way and Watling Street.

Right: **The important public buildings in Roman towns: 1** forum (market place); **2** temple; **3** circus (stadium); **4** baths; **5** theatre. The town wall defences had four main gates **6**.

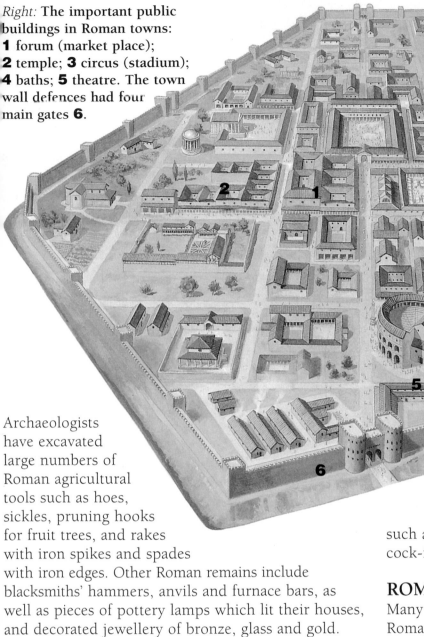

Archaeologists have excavated large numbers of Roman agricultural tools such as hoes, sickles, pruning hooks for fruit trees, and rakes with iron spikes and spades with iron edges. Other Roman remains include blacksmiths' hammers, anvils and furnace bars, as well as pieces of pottery lamps which lit their houses, and decorated jewellery of bronze, glass and gold.

ROMAN TOWN LIFE

The roads were vital military and trade routes in Roman Britain, linking the fortified Roman towns of London, York, Chester, Lincoln and St Albans. The Romans built new towns or converted Celtic bases, introducing proper drains and straight streets that intersected one another at right angles like streets in a modern American city. At the centre of the town was the forum or market place, with a basilica or town hall, and a temple and public baths close by.

The public baths were places for people to meet together to gossip, to do sports or discuss business, rather than simply to wash. The baths were cheap and children got in free. The Romans also built theatres and amphitheatres in several British towns such as St Albans. In these huge arenas, a variety of different shows were put on to amuse the people such as gladiators fighting each other to the death, cock-fighting and bull-baiting.

ROMAN COUNTRY LIFE

Many Britons did not change their way of life under Roman rule. In the countryside, they continued to live in round timber-framed houses and farm much as they had done before the invasion, supporting their families. Because life in the countryside was largely unchanged, archaeologists call the inhabitants of Roman Britain Romano-British (rather than Roman) and that is the name given to things they made and built.

An important change in the British countryside was the Roman villa. Not unlike the stately homes of later centuries, these were large, luxurious houses surrounded by a big estate. They often had mosaic floors and painted walls, and some had glass windows. There would be several bedrooms, living rooms and a large kitchen. Some had central heating (*hypocausts*) with hot water running under the floors.

Above: **The Chi-Ro mosaic at Lullingstone in Kent shows the Christian sign: two Greek letters Chi and Ro – CHR – which stands for *Christos*, or Christ, in Greek. Christianity was brought to Britain by the Romans.**

- AD **60** Romans conquer Anglesey, stronghold of the Druids. Revolt of Boudicca

- AD **81** Julius Agricola reaches the Firth of Forth and establishes northern frontier

- AD **84** Agricola defeats the Picts in the Highlands

- AD **123** Emperor Hadrian builds his great wall on Tyne-Solway line

- AD **143** Romans build Antonine Wall from Firth of Forth to the River Clyde

- AD **163** Romans withdraw south to Hadrian's Wall

- AD **208** Emperor Septimius Severus arrives; invades Caledonia (Scotland)

- AD **211** Severus dies at York

- AD **280** Saxon pirate raids

- AD **284** Emperor Diocletian makes Britain part of the Prefecture of Gaul (France)

- AD **287** St Alban martyred for sheltering a fugitive Christian

- AD **314** Bishops from Lincoln, London and York attend Council of Arles (assembly of the Church of Rome)

Below: **A Roman coin found at Richborough, in Kent, dated AD 410. A Briton cowers before a fully armed Roman soldier on horseback. Richborough was Julius Caesar's chief port and military base.**

DECLINE OF THE EMPIRE

The Romans had to keep soldiers in Britain all the time to guard it against attack. From about AD 280 onwards, Saxon pirates (from what is now Germany) began raiding the shores of Britain. In the north, the Picts were ready to pour over Hadrian's Wall at the least sign of weakness in the Roman defence .

To guard against the Saxon raids, the Romans built a chain of forts along the shores from Norfolk to the Isle of Wight. The forts were under the command of an officer known as the Count of the Saxon Shore. The forts had massive walls, several of which still stand today. Burgh Castle in Norfolk has a fine example of such a wall. These forts held off the raiders until AD 367 when the Picts, the Saxons and warriors from northern Ireland joined forces. These invaders broke through Hadrian's Wall, and killed the Count of the Saxon Shore. But the Romans gradually restored order and made treaties with some of the northern tribes.

THE END OF ROMAN RULE

Two things combined to bring about the end of Roman rule in Britain. One was civil war between rival generals fighting to become emperor. The other was the increasing number of attacks on Rome by barbarian tribes from northern Europe. Slowly, legions of troops were withdrawn from Britain to protect other parts of the Roman empire. The last legion left in AD 406. Four years later, when the Romano-British appealed for help against other foreign invaders, the emperor could only reply: "Take steps to defend yourselves". Roman coins stopped being used by AD 430; Hadrian's Wall and other forts were neglected and villas abandoned; nobody repaired the roads; and 400 years of Roman rule in Britain slowly disappeared.

ROMAN CHRISTIANITY

Christianity was probably brought to Britain by Roman soldiers or civilian settlers from Gaul some time before AD 200. The influence of Roman Christianity led to the building of crosses and later churches. Saxon and British pagan gods and goddesses were slowly replaced. In AD 287 Alban, a Romano-Briton living at Verulamium, sheltered a Christian fleeing from persecution, and was put to death. (Verulamium is now known by its present name of St Albans.)

The Emperor Constantine made Christianity Rome's official religion in AD 324, by which time England already had three bishops, at Lincoln, London and York.

Left: **A Roman pot made in about AD 200 shows men fighting. One holds up a finger to show he has lost. Some pots were made of bronze or iron and others of terracotta (clay). Most pottery was made for table use as platters, bowls or drinking cups.**

ST PATRICK AND THE IRISH

Ireland's first great leader was Cormac, who ruled over Meath and Connacht from AD 275 to 300. He made himself *Ard-Rí* (high king), and set up a national assembly at Tara Hill, in Meath. Even more powerful was Niall of the Nine Hostages, who was high king from AD 380 to 405. At around this time a 16-year-old Romano-British boy, Patrick, was carried off to pagan Ireland and made a slave. He escaped and trained as a Christian priest. About 30 years later he went back to

Ireland as a bishop and a missionary. There were already a few Christians in Ireland, but Patrick's preaching converted almost all of the island. Many legends grew up about Patrick, for instance he is supposed to have banished all the snakes from Ireland. (In fact snakes never reached Ireland after the Ice Age. Ireland became an island at a time when Britain was still attached to the European mainland.) Patrick is the patron saint of Ireland.

Left: **The empire is dismantled. The Romans left in AD 406 and the Romano-British abandoned their country villas. Local farmers took away the valuable materials.**

- ● AD **324** Christianity becomes official religion of Roman empire

- ● AD **325** British bishops attend Council of Nicaea, first world-wide council of Christian Church

- ● AD **366** Picts raid as far south as London.

- ● AD **367** Roman general Theodosius drives the Picts north beyond Hadrian's Wall

- ● AD **401** St Patrick sold into slavery in Ireland by pirates

- ● AD **406** Last Roman legion leaves Britain

- ● AD **407** Romano-Briton Constantine proclaims himself emperor

- ● AD **410** Emperor Honorius tells Romano-Britons that Rome can no longer defend them.

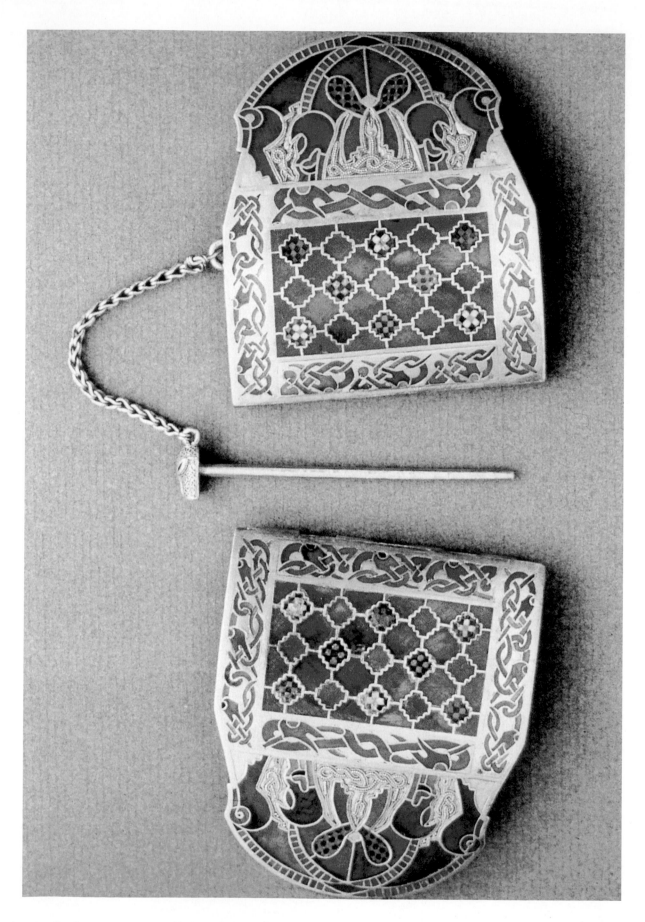

The Anglo-Saxons were skilled metal workers, as this beautifully finished gold shoulder clasp shows.

THE ANGLO-SAXONS
(440 – 1066)

THE ROMAN EMPIRE SPLIT in two – the Western Roman empire and the Eastern (Byzantine) empire. In AD 476 the Western Roman empire collapsed, and the years after this are often known as the Dark Ages. This is partly because so little is known about what happened at that time, and partly because the end of Roman law and order also led to the loss of classical culture, science and learning. The Dark Ages began in Britain much earlier than in the rest of Europe, when the last of the Roman legions left in AD 406. The soldiers were recalled to defend their empire, which was under threat from barbarian invasion, and they were never to return.

By that time Britain was already being attacked by Saxon pirates. The attacks grew stronger and more frequent. For a time the Romano-British people fought them off. Stories of that grim struggle are contained in the legends of King Arthur. But it was the pirate raiders who eventually won. Saxons, Jutes and Angles invaded Britain from northern Germany. From the Angles comes the word Angleland – England.

Later invaders were the Northmen, the fierce Vikings who settled in northern and eastern England and left their mark in place names containing old Norse words like *by*, a village, or *thwaite*, a clearing.

The Anglo-Saxons

EVEN BEFORE THE ROMANS left Britain in AD 406, England was being raided by Saxon pirates as well as by Jutes and Angles attacking from northern Germany, Denmark and what is now Holland and Belgium. The Picts from Scotland also broke through Hadrian's Wall and raided England.

Some Romano-British chiefs fought off these raiders with their own armies. Others invited mercenaries (paid soldiers) to help them fight their enemies. According to legend, the first German mercenaries to come to Britain and wage war on the Romano-British were Hengist and Horsa. The Anglo-Saxons (as we call the Saxons, Angles and Jutes) drove off the Picts, but instead of going back to their homeland they took over the Romano-British kingdoms by force.

- **450** Treasure buried at Mildenhall, Suffolk (found 1942)

- **476** Goths conquer Rome: end of Western Roman empire

- **477** Saxons arrive in England in force

- *c.* **500** Saxons defeated at Badon Hill by Britons under King Arthur

Below: **This map shows the borders of the various Anglo-Saxon tribes in England after the fall of the Roman empire. The Romano-Britons fled to Cornwall, while Wales and most of Scotland remained independent.**

THE DARK AGES AND KING ARTHUR

The years following the collapse of the Roman empire in AD 476 are often known as the Dark Ages, partly because there is so little written history of the time to shed any light on what happened in this period. In many ways it was like a return to life in the Iron Age, before organized Roman rule.

At the time of the fall of the Roman empire there was certainly a Romano-British tribe leader called Arthur who fought the Saxons from about 470 to 500. He lived in a castle called Camelot (it may have been in south Somerset) and he was probably a *dux bellorum*, or commander-in-chief of an army. His most famous victory was at Badon Hill. The legends of Merlin the magician, the sword Excalibur, Guinevere, Lancelot and the Knights of the Round Table are exciting stories but not history. The Round Table at the Great Hall in Winchester is a Tudor reconstruction.

LIFE UNDER THE ANGLO-SAXONS

The Anglo-Saxons built simple wooden houses and barns and made towns into centres for trade and manufacturing. Craftworkers made pottery and glass, and metal workers included skilled jewellers. Most people were farmers, growing barley, oats and wheat for food, and flax for making linen for clothing. Sheep were kept for their wool as much as for their meat, and the Saxons also kept cattle, pigs and goats.

Under each tribal king there were three classes: noblemen; churls, who were freemen or yeomen, many of them owning land; and slaves. A slave could be bought for the price of eight oxen.

Left: **This is a picture for the month of March from an Anglo-Saxon calendar showing the Saxons working the land.**

From about 450 to 650 the Saxons created new kingdoms such as East Anglia (the kingdom of the East Angles), Kent, Sussex, Wessex, Northumbria and Mercia (present-day Midlands). The ancient Britons fled to Cornwall and Brittany in northern France (from where this region gets its name). Mercia was ruled by King Offa from 757 to 796. A strong ruler with a strong army, he is best known for Offa's Dyke, a defence stretching from the Severn estuary to the Irish Sea to keep out the Welsh. Almost 180 kilometres of earthworks 1.5 metres deep were built with wooden barriers and forts at the top. It can still be seen today. The Anglo-Saxons spoke Old English, which has developed into present-day English.

CELTIC AND ROMAN CHRISTIANS

The Romano-Britons were Christians whereas the Anglo-Saxons were pagans who worshipped their own gods and goddesses. St Patrick's followers Columba and Aidan converted the Anglo-Saxons after the Romans had left. They brought Christianity to Scotland and the north of England. There are Celtic monasteries at Iona in Argyll, Scotland and at Lindisfarne on Holy Island off the Northumberland coast. At Tintagel, Cornwall, lies the oldest known monastery in Britain, built by Celtic Christian monks in 470. In 597 Augustine, a missionary sent from Rome by Pope Gregory I to convert England, arrived in Kent and set up a Roman Christian church at Canterbury, where the cathedral would be built.

During the Dark Ages, Celtic and Roman Christians argued fiercely about the form their Church should take. In 664 King Oswy of Northumbria, who had supported Aidan, called a synod (conference) at Whitby, in Yorkshire. There the Celtic Church leaders under the Abbess Hilda decided to follow the Church of Rome and accept the Pope as their leader like the rest of Europe. They also decided on the date of Easter and issues such as the style of a monk's haircut.

Left: **When Saxon soldiers reported that it was safe to land in Britain, whole families arrived. They beached their boats and waded ashore with their sheep and cattle.**

Above: **This elaborate Saxon helmet was crafted of iron, bronze and silver in about 625. It may have belonged to a king of the East Angles.**

MONKS AND LEARNING

Much of what we know about Britain comes from the writings of monks. One of the most important sources is the *History of the English Church and People*, completed in Latin in 731 by the Venerable Bede. He was a monk at the great monastery of Jarrow, near Newcastle, where he taught and wrote. Because he set up a school there for 600 monks, he is referred to as the father of English learning. Bede's *History of the English Church and People* was later translated into Anglo-Saxon by Alfred the Great.

In the monastery of Whitby, Caedmon, a monk who was perhaps the first English (or Saxon) poet, wrote *The Creation*, the earliest surviving English poem. Caedmon is thought of as the founder of English poetry. The other major work of this time is the *Anglo-Saxon Chronicle*, begun in the 800s by monks at Winchester, who recorded important events in England in the Anglo-Saxon language.

THE VIKINGS ATTACK

In the late 700s Northmen, or Norsemen, pirates from Scandinavia, began attacking the Anglo-Saxons. These Northmen were known as Vikings, from a Norse word meaning pirate or sea raider. The monks who wrote the *Anglo-Saxon Chronicle* called them "the heathen" or "the force".

The Vikings sailed in longships, sleek and fast all-weather vessels. They were disciplined fighters, but in their raids they slaughtered, burned and robbed. They carried off the most beautiful women, and took men to sell as slaves. They conquered Northumbria, East Anglia and Mercia. Only Wessex held out against them.

KENNETH MACALPIN, KING OF THE SCOTS

The early inhabitants of Scotland formed a number of tribes. By the 600s these tribes had united to form two kingdoms: Pictavia (land of the Picts), who occupied most of the northern part; and Dalriada (land of the Scots), who had moved to Scotland from Ireland.

In 843 Kenneth MacAlpin (son of Alpin), King of the Scots, claimed the throne of Pictavia through his grandmother, who was a Pictish princess. From his time onwards all the land north of the Clyde-Forth line was united and is now Scotland.

Right: **In the Dark Ages, monks were the only scholars. They copied books to send to other monasteries.**

KING EGBERT

During this time, a new dynasty of rulers was begun by Egbert, King of Wessex, who reigned from 802 to 839. He became the first king who could claim to be ruler over all England. Egbert enlarged Wessex (which at this point consisted of Berkshire, Devon, Dorset, Hampshire, Somerset, Wiltshire) to include Kent, Sussex, Surrey and Cornwall.

Egbert defeated Offa's powerful kingdom of Mercia at the battle of Ellandun in 825 (at Wroughton in Wiltshire). After this victory the people of Mercia and Northumbria acknowledged Egbert as Bretwalda (Lord of Britain). Egbert's grandson was Alfred the Great.

ALFRED THE GREAT

The Vikings who invaded England in the mid-800s came from Denmark, so we also call them Danes. They conquered Northumbria, took York and East Anglia, and overran Mercia. They would have conquered the whole of England but for the efforts of Alfred the Great. Alfred was the youngest son of King Ethelwulf of Wessex. He had spent much of his youth in Rome, where he was educated.

Above: **Egbert (775-839). After being banished for laying claim to the West Saxon kingship, Egbert later returned to become King of Wessex in 802, and first ruler of England.**

Below: **The Vikings, or Danes, were bold sailors and fearsome soldiers. Their main weapons were swords, axes and spears.**

ALFRED DEFEATS THE DANES

During his fierce resistence of the Danes, Alfred spent some months hiding in the Isle of Athelney, among the marshes of Somerset. It is from here that the legend arose of Alfred burning cakes and being scolded by a local swineherd who did not recognize him as king.

In 871 Alfred defeated the Danes at the battle of Ashdown on the Berkshire Downs. He sought a peace in which the Danes agreed not to attack Wessex in return for a payment called the Danegeld – meaning gold for the Danes. But after five years the Danes under King Guthrum again attacked Wessex. Alfred raised an army and defeated the Danes at the battle of Edington in Wiltshire in 878. He also forced the King Guthrum to sign the Treaty of Wedmore and be baptized.

THE DANELAW

A new frontier between Wessex and the Danish territory followed the line of Watling Street, the old Roman road which ran from London to Chester. Alfred allowed the Danes to settle in the lands to the east of Watling Street, in what was later called the Danelaw. The Danes have left us their words such as *loft* (as in Lowestoft) meaning 'farmhouse' and *thorpe* (as in Scunthorpe) which means 'village'. In 890, Alfred built a fleet of ships to defend the shores of his southern kingdom of England. He also founded several new fortified towns, called *burhs*.

Right: **By the Treaty of Wedmore in 878, Alfred let the Danes take over eastern England as the Danelaw.**

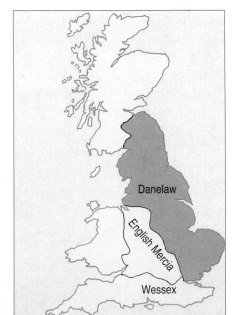

Danelaw

English Mercia

Wessex

- **540** Bubonic plague in Britain
- **563** St Columba founds Iona monastery in western Scotland
- **590** Gregory I, the Great, becomes Pope (to 604)
- **597** St Augustine founds a monastery at Canterbury
- **600** Saxons, Angles and Jutes control most of England
- **604** First church of St Paul, London
- **613** Northumbrians defeat Britons near Chester
- **624-625** Sutton Hoo ship burial
- **627** Bishop Paulinus converts Edwin of Northumbria to Christianity and becomes Archbishop of York
- **635** Lindisfarne monastery established. St Aidan Bishop of Northumbria
- **642** Oswald of Northumbria killed in battle against Penda of Mercia
- **650** Epic poem Beowulf written
- **664** Synod of Whitby: Roman form of worship chosen over Celtic
- **704** Ethelred of Mercia abdicates to become a monk
- **716** Ethelbald becomes King of Mercia (to 747)
- **731** Venerable Bede completes History of the English Church and People
- **750** Gregorian chants first sung in England
- **757** Offa becomes King of Mercia (to 796)
- **760** Book of Kells written in Ireland
- **772-775** Offa builds Offa's Dyke defence to keep out the Welsh

17

Left: **The Alfred Jewel, set in gold and crystal with a miniature enamel portrait of the king. It bears the Saxon words for "Alfred ordered me to be made". This may have been the decorated end of a bookmark, to be used by a priest or monk when reading the Bible. Alfred was a religious man and encouraged his people to go to church.**

- **787** Vikings raid Wessex
- **794** Vikings raid Scottish isles
- **795** First Viking raid on Ireland
- **802** Egbert is King of Wessex (to 839); Mercia's dominance is challenged
- **834** Kenneth MacAlpin becomes King of the Scots
- **843** MacAlpin defeats the Picts and unites Picts and Scots
- **856** Ethelwulf dies; succeeded by Ethelbald (to 860), Ethelbert (to 865) and Ethelred (to 871)
- **869** Danes occupy East Anglia and kill St Edmund
- **871** Alfred the Great becomes King of Wessex (to 899)
- **878** Alfred defeats Danes; Treaty of Wedmore divides England between Danes (Danelaw) and Saxons
- **890** Alfred establishes navy
- **891** Anglo-Saxon Chronicle begun
- **900** England divided into shires
- **919** Danes triumph in Dublin
- **980** Danes begin almost yearly raids on Britain

Above: **In Alfred the Great's time England was divided into many small kingdoms.**

Right: **A statue of Alfred the Great stands at Wantage in Oxfordshire, his birthplace. Alfred was devout and scholarly. He translated several works from Latin into Old English.**

THE WESSEX KINGS

Three kings, Alfred, Edward the Elder and Athelstan made the Anglo-Saxon kingdom of England strong. Alfred's son, Edward the Elder, defeated the Danes several times in his 25-year reign, and ruled over all of England south of the river Humber. The Danelaw settlers of East Anglia and the Midlands submitted to him, and the Welsh princes also acknowledged him as their overlord. Edward's son, Athelstan, defeated a coalition of Vikings, Scots and Irish Celts at the battle of Brunanburh (937).

But a succession of weak rulers lost these gains. The weakest was Ethelred II, who came to the throne in 978, aged ten. Ethelred was known as the *Unraed - redeless*, or evil-counselled. The word was later translated as "unready". The Danes began raiding again and inflicted a defeat over the Saxons at the battle of Maldon in Essex, in 991. Ethelred was ill-advised to use the Danegeld (as Alfred had done at first) to try to buy off the Danes with bribes. Eventually his kingdom shrank to just Wessex and Kent.

Ethelred then attacked the Danes who were living peacefully in Wessex, including Gunhilda, sister of the Danish King Sweyn. Infuriated, the Danes waged war until, in 1013, they proclaimed Sweyn King of England. Ethelred fled to Normandy in France, the home of his wife, Emma. Their marriage established the first dynastic link between England and Normandy.

THE DANISH KINGS

Sweyn died in 1014, one year after becoming King of England. Ethelred came back, but he died in 1016. His son, Edmund Ironside, and Sweyn's son, Canute, battled for the throne. They finally agreed to share the kingdom between them, but Edmund died suddenly, having ruled his portion for just seven months.

Canute now became king of all England. He was also king of much of Scandinavia including Denmark, Norway and southern Sweden, but wisely he chose Englishmen for the Church and for his Court.

Right: **The Danes who moved to Britain were farming people. They lived in simple wooden houses and cleared the forests for land.**

KING CANUTE

Canute brought peace and prosperity to England. He supplied a firm, fair government and maintained an army. Canute said: "I have vowed to God to govern my kingdoms with equity, and to act justly in all things". Two of his sons succeeded him as kings from 1035 to 1042: Harold I, known as Harefoot, and Harthacanute. Neither king contributed to the country's development.

THE LAST SAXON KINGS

In 1042, Edward, son of Ethelred II and Emma of Normandy, became king. Although he was a Saxon he had been brought up in Normandy and learned Norman ways. He was so devout that his people called him Edward the Confessor. Westminster Abbey was begun during his reign in 1052. Edward died in 1066 after naming his brother-in-law Harold Godwinsson, Earl of Wessex, as his heir. The Witan, the Saxon council, agreed and he was crowned Harold II at Westminster Abbey on January 6, 1066, the last Saxon king of England.

Left: **Edward the Confessor (1042-1066) elder son of Ethelred the Unready and Emma, daughter of Richard, Duke of the Normans. Edward founded Westminster Abbey.**

Above: **King Canute was surrounded by courtiers who tried to win his favour by flattery. There is a story that, to prove he was not taken in by their flattery, he commanded the tide to turn back – and got wet. Clearly even a king was less powerful than God and the forces of nature.**

- **1005** Malcolm II becomes King of Scotland (to 1034)

- **1013** Danes control England. Sweyn proclaimed King of England

- **1016** Canute, son of Sweyn becomes King of England

- **1034** Duncan I is King of Scotland

- **1035** Canute dies; succeeded by son, Harold I (Harefoot)

- **1040** Harold I dies; succeeded by half brother Harthacanute (to 1042). Macbeth kills Duncan I in battle, and becomes King of Scotland (to 1057)

- **1042** Edward, Ethelred II's son, becomes king (to 1066)

- **1057-1058** Duncan's son Malcolm kills Macbeth, and becomes Malcolm III King of Scots

- **1064** Harold Godwinsson shipwrecked in Normandy; forced to swear allegiance to William, Duke of Normandy, before William will release him

- **1066** Edward dies; Harold Godwinsson crowned last Saxon king of England

A beautiful book cover drawn by monks at Kells in Ireland. At the time of the Norman invasion, these monks lived in a monastery with beehive-shaped huts, a central stone chapel and a five-storey round tower.

THE NORMANS
(1066 – 1154)

IN THE 600 YEARS SINCE the Saxon pirates began to settle amid the ruins of the old Roman province of Britain, their descendants had made England one of the wealthiest and best-governed lands in western Europe. The Danes had also finally settled peacefully in the country. All was about to change, however, because the Anglo-Saxon king, Edward the Confessor, had no son to take his place. The storm clouds were gathering. Once again the Northmen threatened. Harald Hardrada of Norway, aided by Tostig, the renegade Earl of Northumbria, was waiting to pounce. So too were William, Duke of Normandy, who was Edward's brother-in-law, and named heir Harold Godwinsson, Earl of Wessex, who was Tostig's brother.

William won the contest, and for the next hundred years England was ruled by Norman kings. The Normans brought about a major change – they ended England's isolation. Henceforth England was very much a part of Europe. Indeed, until 1558, English monarchs owned a part of France – at times the major part.

Scotland and Ireland retained their independence under the Norman kings. Wales already had links with the Saxon kings, and within a few years the Normans overran southern Wales, but for centuries northern Wales remained independent of the Normans.

The Normans

THE NORMANS WERE originally Vikings who had settled in northwest France in the early 900s, by the River Seine. In 1066 an army of up to 7,000 men crossed over the English Channel in hundreds of boats.

CONTENDERS FOR THE CROWN

This invasion was led by William, Duke of Normandy, who claimed that he was the rightful King of England, even though Harold Godwinsson had already been crowned king and accepted by the Witan. King Harold led the English army to oppose the Norman invasion. But he and many of his men were weary. Three weeks earlier they had fought and beaten Harald Hardrada, a Norwegian contender for the throne, at Stamford Bridge in Yorkshire, and then had a six-day forced march back to London. Now Harold's forces assembled on the Sussex downs, near the town of Battle.

Left: **William I, the Conqueror (1066-1087) was the illegitimate son of Robert, Duke of Normandy. He defeated Harold, King of England, at the battle of Hastings in 1066 and was crowned king. He was a stern but efficient ruler.**

Above: **The charge of the Normans at the battle of Hastings. The Normans were more heavily armed than their Saxon opponents.**

Below: **Part of the famous Bayeux Tapestry telling the story of William's conquest. The pictures are embroidered in different coloured wool.**

- **1066** Edward the Confessor dies; Witan offers throne to Harold II; Tostig and Harald Hardrada of Norway invade northern England; defeated at Stamford Bridge by Harold. William of Normandy invades Sussex; defeats and kills Harold at Hastings. Halley's Comet seen

- **1070** Malcolm III invades Northumbria. Lanfranc Archbishop of Canterbury. Hereward the Wake heads a rising in fen country

- **1071** William I subdues fen rebellion

- **1072** William raids Scotland. Normans conquer Sicily in the Mediterranean

- **1073** Lincoln Cathedral begun

- **1078** Tower of London begun. Pope Gregory VII sends legates to reorganize Church in England

- **1079** William's son Robert Curthose begins castle that gives Newcastle-upon-Tyne its name

- **1086** Domesday Book completed

- **1087** William dies at Rouen. William II becomes king. Robert becomes Duke of Normandy

TRAN · SIVIT · ETVE

THE BATTLE OF HASTINGS

The Saxons and Normans were closely matched and the battle of Hastings lasted eight hours, a long time for a medieval battle. The best-armed Saxons (the *thegns* and king's bodyguards) formed a shield-wall against the Norman knights and infantry. The opposing armies met at Hastings on October 14, 1066. The English fought on foot with Harold fighting between his two brothers. They fought off several attacks by Normans on horseback. The Normans then pretended to retreat and some of Harold's forces, thinking they had won the battle, chased after them breaking up their shield-wall. Norman archers then fired arrows over them with deadly effect. According to legend, Harold was pierced through the eye by a Norman arrow, and killed.

William of Normandy advanced to Dover, then to Coventry and finally to London. On Christmas Day 1066, he was crowned King of England.

WILLIAM THE CONQUEROR

The man who overthrew the Saxons, known ever since as William the Conqueror, was the illegitimate son of Duke Robert of Normandy and a tanner's daughter, Arlette. William was only seven when Robert died. Life was hard for any young boy expected to be a duke. It was much worse for a son born out of marriage. By the time he was 20, William had put down one major rebellion by his barons, and he would have to overcome many more.

THE DOMESDAY BOOK

William subdued England by taking the land away from the Anglo-Saxon lords and giving it to his Norman barons. He ordered many wooden and later stone castles to be built to protect his rule, and also sent out men to record what was in his new kingdom. The survey, recorded in the Domesday Book, was carried out in the first seven months of 1086 and showed that the population was about one and a half million. Every manor and land holding was recorded. William could now check that none of his noblemen had seized other property, and exactly what rents and fees their land should bear. Domesday comes from the word *dom*, meaning assessment. It was so thorough that, as the monks of the *Anglo-Saxon Chronicle* commented: "There was not a single hide nor rod of land ... not an ox, a cow, a pig was left out".

Left: **The Domesday Book is normally associated with Winchester where it was most probably compiled. It was actually two books: the first volume of 382 pages describes most of the country while the second volume was called Little Domesday, and was possibly compiled by monks at Ely.**

FOCUS ON NORMAN CATHEDRALS

The Normans brought over their architects from the Continent, who helped plan big Romanesque churches and cathedrals such as at Chichester and Durham. Romanesque was a style of western European architecture from the 10th to 13th centuries which featured ribbed vaulting and rounded arches. Deep doorways had rounded arches supported by thick, strong pillars and with highly decorated mouldings. The windows were often bordered with a chevron or a V-shape. Norman builders had only simple equipment with which to build their great cathedrals and churches, but the results were spectacular.

Domesday Village Life

VILLAGE LIFE revolved around the parish church because it was the only public building. The church and churchyard were used for fairs and games as well as for religious services and festivals such as Christmas, Whitsun and Easter. Sundays and Mondays were usually days of rest.

Most village people were *villeins*, who owned a few plough oxen and a small piece of land called a small-holding. They had to farm on the lord of the manor's land for certain amounts of time, and then at other times they could cultivate their own strips of land and tend to their livestock. Below villeins were the *bordars* who owned even less land (about two hectares) and had no livestock.

There were often one or two manors in a village and the barons owned all the large open fields, with some of the peasants being allowed to own much smaller strips of land. Any meadow or woodland was also owned by the barons. Manors varied greatly in size, ranging from many square kilometres to just a few hectares.

Farming was mainly hard manual work – sowing, weeding and harvesting were all done by hand. Only ploughing was aided by oxen. Sheep were the most important livestock, and often those belonging to villagers outnumbered those owned by the manor. Sheep were raised for their meat, for their wool (which could be sold by the owners), and for cheese made from their milk. At harvest time the lord of the manor would

Right: **An artist's impression of what a typical baron's manor would have looked like. The manor was a fortified home and it would have included a castle 1 for a lookout and protection. The baron himself would have lived in the large thatched building 2 inside a defensive picket fence called a bailey 3. The farm buildings 4 include barns, a blacksmith's shop and the bailiff's (farm manager) house. The villeins' houses 5 are grouped away from the baron's castle, around the parish church 6. There are three fields for farming: one for wheat 7, one for barley or oats 8 and one left fallow 9. This baron also has a deer park 10, a vineyard 11, and an orchard 12.**

provide pork, chicken, cabbages, eggs, cheese and apples for those gathering the crops.

In the autumn many farm animals were killed and their meat preserved in salt. This saved on precious winter fodder and also meant the villagers had a source of nourishment during the long winter months. They ate fish on Fridays and Holy Days as the Church did not allow them to eat meat on these days. The manor also ran the water-mill for grinding the manor's and the villagers' corn. There were also fisheries on the rivers, with part of the catch paid to the lord of the manor. Hunting was reserved for the Norman lords who created areas of countryside in which deer and boars could roam.

Above: **A house belonging to a tenant called a bordar. He was one of the lowest tenants in the feudal structure of land ownership and loyalty to the lord of the manor. This house has a timber frame filled in with wattle and daub (which is mud and plaster on a wicker mesh). It is built close to a wood and would have a run for pigs reared in the woods and fed on acorns. After sheep, pigs were the most important livestock, and the Domesday Book often described woods by the number of pigs that could be kept in them. Women worked as hard in the village as men, helping them in the fields, making baskets, plucking geese for arrow-feathers, stitching sheepskin for saddle-bags and churning butter – all duties performed for the manor house. At home, women would look after their children, house and garden.**

The Feudal System

UNDER WHAT IS CALLED the feudal system, which the Normans brought with them from France, all the land in England was owned by the king. He allowed others to hold some of it in return for certain services. The Domesday Book reveals what was owned by the king and through him, by his barons. These barons had private armies, under the command of knights, who were meant to be ready to fight for the king whenever he wanted them to do so. The barons built castles for defence and lived in manor houses.

HOW FEUDALISM BEGAN

After the collapse of the Roman empire, around the year AD 476, law and order had crumbled in Europe and barbarians invaded from all sides. The feudal system grew out of this lawlessness. It began in France, in about AD 750, and soon spread across Europe.

Fearing for their lives, people banded together under the protection of strong leaders or kings. But no leader was strong enough on his own to resist attack or control fighting between local barons, so the king granted land to certain powerful barons, in return for their promising to help him fight his enemies and pay him taxes.

HOW THE FEUDAL SYSTEM WORKED

The feudal system was based on exchanging land for services rather than for rent. The term comes from the Latin for fief, *feudum,* which means any land given away. At the top were the barons and Church institutions who held land given to them by the king and were called tenants-in-chief. In return for this land they were expected to pay the king taxes and provide him with knights to help him fight his enemies. William tried to ensure that the barons' estates were scattered about the country so their power was diluted.

The barons kept some land for themselves and also allowed their knights to hold some of their land. Knights were trained warriors. In exchange for land, each knight had to promise to follow his baron to war or guard his castle for 40 days in a year, and provide a certain number of soldiers.

Left: **William I made all landowners swear loyalty only to him. This meant they could not swear loyalty to powerful barons who might then build up private armies against the king. William also introduced the practice of knight service, whereby each knight had to follow the baron to war or guard his castle, for 40 days each year. In turn, the baron pledged allegiance to the king.**

Below the knights in the feudal system came yeomen, or farmers, who were all free men. They usually lived in a village near the manor house and had to work a few days a week for the baron. At the lowest level were the peasants, known as serfs, who provided the baron with crops in return for protection. Serfs belonged to the baron, as property. They could be bought or sold, as could their children. They could not leave the village or get married without the baron's permission. They did not own their land. This series of arrangements was the basis of what is called the feudal system.

Right: **The feudal system created a definite hierarchy, from the powerful at the top to the poorest at the bottom. First came the clergy, then the knight and his family, who were loyal to a baron. The middle class of merchants, lawyers, and yeoman farmers did not owe any services to a baron – they were free, as were craftworkers and shopkeepers. At the bottom were footsoldiers and the serfs.**

FOCUS ON THE TOWER OF LONDON

As soon as the Normans moved into an area they would build a wooden fort, usually on a high earth mound with the garrison below protected by high wooden ramparts. The site would be carefully chosen because it overlooked the neighbouring countryside or it dominated a river or important overland route.

No castle could be built without the king's permission – another way of keeping the feudal system working and the barons in check. The most famous castle was the White Tower, built in London to protect the city from enemies coming up the Thames. The White Tower started out as a simple timber-and-earth castle built a few months after the victory at Hastings. By 1100 it was a large 28 metre stone tower with rooms for the royal family, surrounded by wooden buildings for the army and administrators. Today, the White Tower is known by its more famous name: the Tower of London – once the main residence for all English kings from William II to Henry VII. It was also to become a royal mint, a prison, a place of execution and a home for the Crown Jewels and Royal Armoury. The Royal Armoury was moved to Leeds in 1996.

- **1089** William II campaigns to take Normandy from his brother

- **1090** Most of Wales comes under Norman rule. Ely and Norwich cathedrals begun

- **1092** William takes Cumbria from Scots

- **1093** Anselm of Bec becomes Archbishop of Canterbury. Malcolm III of Scotland killed while invading England: Donald Bane succeeds him. Durham Cathedral begun

- **1094** Revolt in northwest Wales. Duncan II, son of Malcolm III, drives out Donald Bane, but is later killed

- **1095** Anselm quarrels with William and goes to Rome.

- **1096** First Crusade begins. Normans conquer south Wales. William lends Robert funds for a crusade in return for keeping Normandy as a loan

- **1097** Edgar, son of Malcolm III, deposes and succeeds Donald Bane (to 1107); he accepts William as his overlord. Revolt by the Welsh

- **1099** William holds his first court at Westminster. He conquers Maine in north France

- **1100** William II killed while hunting; succeeded by Henry I (to 1135). Henry marries Matilda, daughter of Malcolm III of Scotland

- **1101** Robert of Normandy, back from the crusades, invades England, but is bought off

- **1106** Henry I defeats and captures Robert at battle of Tinchebrai, and gains Normandy

- **1107** Synod of Westminster: Henry gives up his right to choose bishops and abbots, and is reconciled with Anselm

- **1109** Anselm dies. Henry at war with France

WILLIAM II – THE RED KING

William the Conqueror died from injuries he suffered following a riding accident in 1087. He left Normandy to his eldest son, Robert, and England to his younger but more tough-minded son, William. William II was known as Rufus because of his ruddy complexion (Rufus means red in Latin). William II continued his father's strong rule but he was also a cruel king. He taxed his subjects, including the Church, as much as he could. Several times his barons rebelled in support of Robert of Normandy, a gentler man whom they thought would be easier to deal with. William suppressed these revolts with the aid of the *fyrd*, the old Saxon part-time army. He also fought off two invasions from Malcolm III of Scotland. Scotland and Ireland kept their independence under the Norman kings.

William II was fond of hunting stags and while out hunting in the New Forest he was killed by an arrow. It may have been an accident, but some say that Walter Tyrell, who fired the arrow, was acting on orders from William's younger brother, Henry.

Above: **William II, Rufus, (1087-1100) was born in 1066. He had long, red hair, and was hated by his people. He was shot by an arrow while hunting in the New Forest.**

Above: **Henry I (1100-1135) was born in 1068. He seized the throne on the death of Rufus. A strong king, it was said that in his time no man dared to harm another.**

Above: **Ten thousand Norman soldiers were stationed throughout England.**

Left: **With some 70 years of Norman rule and relative peace, towns began to grow. Traders and craftworkers settled in the bigger towns, such as London and Winchester.**

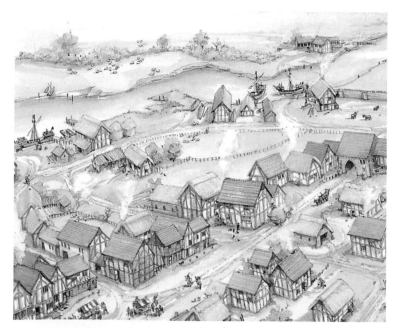

HENRY I

Henry seized the throne and took possession of the royal treasury at Winchester the day after William's death. Robert of Normandy did not accept Henry I as king and the two fought on both sides of the Channel until, in 1106, Henry defeated Robert at the battle of Tinchebrai in Normandy. Robert was imprisoned in England for 28 years until his death. Henry I became known as the Lion of Justice.

THE *CURIA REGIS*

King Henry set up the *Curia Regis,* or King's Council to settle land and other disputes between the king and his tenants. This was the beginning of the Civil Service, the body of officials who help the government run the country.

Henry, who was often absent in Normandy, needed an efficient government to operate in England in his absence. He created a class of loyal administrators from the servants of his royal household, including the chamberlain, who looked after the royal bedchamber; the marshal, who controlled the royal stables; the treasurer; and the steward, who looked after Court officials called ushers. Henry's chancellor, or secretary, issued writs for the sheriffs, or shire-reeves, who administered the counties. The chief officer of the state was the justiciar, who was the equivalent of today's Lord Chief Justice, but also acted as regent, or stand-in, when the king was overseas.

Above: **In 1120, the *White Ship*, carrying Henry I's son, William, struck some rocks and sank in the English Channel. William was drowned.**

THE *WHITE SHIP* DISASTER

Henry I had made himself popular with his Saxon subjects by marrying Edith (also known as Matilda), the daughter of Malcolm III of Scotland and of Margaret, a Saxon princess, herself sister of Edgar Atheling, a Saxon claimant to the throne. In 1120 Henry I's only son, William, and Henry's daughter Adela, were drowned returning from Normandy to England in a vessel called the *White Ship*. Henry was so grief-stricken that, it is said, he was never again seen to smile.

FOCUS ON NORMAN CRAFTWORKERS

Craftworkers such as stone masons and metal workers lived in the towns and sold their goods there. Stone masons carved stone columns and blocks, as well as decorative gargoyles, sometimes with the faces of people they knew! They carved their own special marks on cathedrals, churches and castles to identify

their work. The main crafts were cloth making, leatherwork, carpentry and metalwork. For hundreds of years wool was the main British export to Europe, where it was dyed in vats and woven into cloth. Goldsmiths were also busy and safehouses were provided to keep their priceless ornaments out of the reach of robbers.

Henry had lost his only legitimate son and heir to the throne, so he now tried to persuade his barons to swear to stand by his eldest daughter, Matilda.

Henry's daughter Matilda had been married to Henry V of Germany (who died in 1125). In 1126 the barons agreed to accept her as their next ruler. For greater security Henry I married her to Geoffrey Plantagenet, Count of Anjou.

MATILDA AGAINST STEPHEN

Despite their promises to Henry I, many Norman barons were still reluctant to see his daughter Matilda – or any woman – become the next monarch. Many barons did not like Geoffrey of Anjou because he tried to weaken their power. There was also another contender for the throne: Henry I's nephew, Stephen of Blois, son of William the Conqueror's daughter Adela and the French Count of Blois. He was more likely to let the barons have their own way. In the end the rival claims of Matilda and Stephen of Blois seemed to be decided when Stephen was the first to arrive in London after King Henry died in 1135.

Aided by his brother Henry, Bishop of Winchester, Stephen quickly won the support of the Church, and only three weeks after Henry died he was crowned king. Matilda, however, did not give up her claim to the throne.

STEPHEN'S WEAK REIGN

The Normans had provided England with 60 years of firm rule by three strong kings. Stephen, however, was both good natured and weak. Unchecked by a firm king, the Norman barons avoided paying the taxes they owed to the Crown and built castles where they liked, raiding and robbing at random. In total the barons built 100 new baronial castles in defiance of the king. Stephen's disputed claim to the throne also plunged the country into years of civil war. A number of barons went over to Matilda who was supported in her fight for the throne by her half-brother Robert, Earl of Gloucester.

Right: **An impressive Norman castle overlooking its own village, is visited by the king. The lord of the manor or baron was expected to entertain the king and his followers.**

Above: **Matilda was the only daughter of Henry I. Some nobles accepted her as queen in 1141, but most continued to support the weaker Stephen of Blois.**

Above: **Stephen of Blois (1135-1154) was the son of William I's daughter Adela. A weak king, he gained only the contempt of his barons. He was the first English king to allow jousting tournaments.**

- **1110** Henry I betrothes his eight-year-old daughter Matilda to the Holy Roman Emperor, Henry V, and increases taxes for her dowry. Bad weather ruins the crops. Earliest known miracle play performed at Dunstable, Bedfordshire, about this time

- **1114** Henry leads an army into Wales and makes peace. Chichester Cathedral is begun

- **1120** Prince William drowned in the *White Ship* off Harfleur.

- **1121** Henry marries again, to Adela of Louvain

- **1123** Rahere, Henry's jester, founds Augustinian priory of St Bartholomew, London

- **1124** First Scottish coinage

- **1126** Henry persuades barons to accept his daughter Matilda as his heir

- **1128** Widowed Matilda marries again, to Geoffrey Plantagenet, son of Fulk, Count of Anjou. David of Scotland founds Holyrood Abbey, near Edinburgh

- **1129** Fulk goes to Palestine: Geoffrey takes over rule of Anjou, Maine and Touraine.

- **1131** Tintern Abbey founded

- **1133** St Bartholomew's Fair first held at Smithfield (the "smooth field"), London; held once a year for over 700 years

Left: **The layout of the castle would include: 1** a spiral staircase; **2** baron's bedroom; **3** great hall; **4** chapel; **5** kitchen and store rooms.

Robert was the illegitimate son of Henry I, but rather than claim the throne for himself he chose to support his half-sister.

THE SCOTS ATTACK

The Scots under King David joined in the fray and invaded northern England in 1138. They were repelled by an English army hurriedly gathered together by the brave Archbishop of York, Thurstan. His troops carried the banners of St Cuthbert, St John of Beverley and St Wilfred, all much revered in the north. The men of the north, led by Thurstan's clergy, fell on the Scots at Northallerton and killed 12,000 of them. This bloody slaughter is known as the battle of the Standard.

MATILDA TAKES POWER

In 1139, Matilda landed at Portsmouth with Robert and they won many campaigns. In 1141 they captured Stephen at Lincoln Castle and imprisoned him at Bristol Castle. Matilda was made queen, and was acknowledged as Lady of the English by Stephen's own brother, Henry, the Bishop of Winchester. But she imposed many taxes on the English people and once again made the barons hostile to her. Her reign lasted only eight months. Bishop Henry deserted Matilda and rejoined Stephen. Robert was captured and exchanged for Stephen. On Stephen's release the war intensified and Matilda was besieged in Oxford Castle. She escaped in 1142 by disguising herself in a white robe and fleeing through the snow. Eventually she went to Normandy, and never returned.

● **1135** Henry I dies in Normandy. Stephen of Blois, his nephew, crosses to England and seizes the throne. Foundation of Fountains Abbey in Yorkshire

● **1136** Stephen gives Cumberland to David of Scotland, who accepts Stephen as king. Matilda claims the throne

● **1137** Geoffrey of Monmouth writes his largely fictional History of the Kings of Britain. Stephen wins campaign in Normandy against Geoffrey of Anjou

● **1138** Robert, Earl of Gloucester, begins civil war in support of Matilda. David of Scotland supports her, but is defeated at battle of the Standard

● **1141** Battle of Lincoln: Matilda's forces capture Stephen. Stephen's supporters defeat Matilda's army at Winchester, and capture Robert of Gloucester. Stephen and Robert exchanged

● **1142** Matilda escapes from Oxford Castle

● **1144** Geoffrey of Anjou captures Rouen, and controls Normandy

● **1147** Matilda leaves England

● **1149** Matilda's son Henry returns to England; knighted by David I of Scotland

● **1151** Geoffrey of Anjou dies; his son Henry succeeds him.

● **1152** Eleanor marries Henry of Anjou. Synod at Kells; Pope acknowledged as supreme head of the Church in Ireland

● **1153** Henry of Anjou lands in England. Treaty of Wallingford; Stephen agrees Henry shall be his heir. Death of David I of Scotland; succeeded by grandson Malcolm IV (to 1165)

● **1154** Nicholas Breakspear elected as Pope Adrian IV (only English pope). Death of Stephen

THE BARONS REBEL

With the death of Robert in 1147 Matilda lost her only close ally and so she abandoned her claims to the throne. Stephen was confirmed as king, but he still proved quite incapable of controlling the barons. The country remained in disorder. Stephen tried to gain the barons' support with extravagant gifts, but they realized that he was a weak ruler and that they could do as they liked, which they did.

HENRY OF ANJOU

Order was not restored during Stephen's reign until 1153, when a powerful contender for the throne landed in England. His name was Henry, son of Matilda (Henry I's daughter) and of Geoffrey Plantagenet (Count of Anjou). Henry of Anjou had first come to England when he was 11 years old to be educated in Bristol Castle by Robert of Gloucester who was Matilda's half-brother.

Henry's marriage, in 1152, had surprised Europe. His bride was Eleanor of Aquitaine, ruler in her own right of a large part of France as the heir to the Duke of Aquitaine. Henry's possessions in France were already larger than all England, and now, with his wife, he controlled more than half of France.

In 1153 Henry landed in England to claim his right to the throne. Although he could not defeat Stephen decisively, at Wallingford in Oxfordshire he forced Stephen and the barons to accept his terms to end the civil war. Stephen was to keep the throne, but acknowledge Henry as his heir. Stephen, the last of the Norman kings, died in 1154, and Henry II was crowned King of England.

Above: **The four Norman kings. William I and William II are on the top row; Henry I and Stephen are below. The first three kings created strong Norman rule, but Stephen threw it away. Until his reign, Norman rule had helped to develop Britain's economy and end Viking raids.**

Left: **Geoffrey Plantagenet, Count of Anjou, was one of the first people known to have borne a coat-of-arms. It featured the three lions which still appear on the royal arms of England.**

RULERS OF BRITAIN

HOUSE	NAME	REIGN	MARRIED	CHILDREN
WESSEX	Egbert First King of all the English	802 – 839	Raedburh	Ethelwulf
	Ethelwulf	839 – 856	1. Osburh. 2. Judith	Ethelbald, Ethelbert, Ethelred I, and Elfred (Alfred the Great)
	Ethelbald	856 – 860	Judith (his stepmother)	
	Ethelbert	860 – 865		
	Ethelred I	865 – 871		
	Alfred the Great	871 – 899	Ealhswith	Edward the Elder, Ethelfleda
	Edward the Elder	899 – 924	1. Egwina	Ethelstan (Athelstan)
			2. Elfleda	
			3. Edgifu	Edmund I, Edred
	Athelstan	924 – 939		
	Edmund I	939 – 946	Aelfgifu	Edwy, Edgar the Peaceable
	Edred	946 – 955		
	Edwy	955 – 959		
	Edgar the Peaceable	959 – 975	1. Ethelfled	Edward the Martyr
			2. Elfreda	Ethelred II the Unready
	Edward the Martyr	975 – 978		
	Ethelred II, the Unready	978 – 1013	1. Aelfgifu	Edmund II Ironside
		1014 – 1016	2. Emma of Normandy (also married Canute)	Edward the Confessor
DANES	Sweyn	1013 –1014	Gunhilda	Canute
	Edmund II, Ironside	1016	Ealdgyth	Edward
	Canute	1016 – 1035	1. Aelfgifu	Harold I Harefoot,
			2. Emma of Normandy	Harthacanute
	Harold I	1035 – 1040		
	Harthacanute	1040 – 1042		
SAXONS	Edward the Confessor	1042 – 1066	Edith (sister of Harold II)	
	Harold II, Godwinsson (died at the Battle of Hastings)	1066		
NORMANS	William I	1066 – 1087	Matilda of Flanders	Robert, William II, Henry I, Adela (married Count of Blois)
	William II, Rufus	1087 – 1100		
	Henry I	1100 – 1135	1. Edith (Matilda)	William and Adela (drowned on *White Ship*), and Matilda (married Geoffrey of Anjou)
			2. Adela of Louvain	
	Stephen of Blois	1135 – 1154	Matilda of Boulogne	Baldwin, Matilda, Eustace

GLOSSARY

allegiance loyalty to a person or cause

bailiff lord of the manor's chief officer

canonize to formally declare a person a saint. Used by the Roman Catholic Church

besiege to surround a town or castle, cutting off supply lines and attacking with the aim of capturing

Celts Iron Age tribes from Europe

civilization a stage in society when people have developed skills and a way of living together in communities and towns

Holy Roman Empire a federation of European states and princes that lasted from 800 to 1803

hypocaust Roman underfloor central heating system

milecastle fort on Hadrian's Wall – built to station Roman soldiers and officials

monastery residence of a religious male community, bound together by religious vows and living apart from society

mosaic a pattern or picture made of coloured tiles – used to good effect by the Romans on their floors etc

noble person of high birth directly serving the king

pagan a person who follows any pre-Christian religion, especially one with many gods

Picts 'painted people' north of Antonine Wall who periodically harried the Romans

shire county; now only found as part of many county names

slave a person legally owned by another without freedom or rights

Witan the Anglo-Saxon council-meeting of wise men

INDEX

ACKNOWLEDGMENTS

The publishers would like
to thank the following for
supplying additional
illustrations for this book:

Picture research:
Alex Goldberg, Elaine Willis

page 19, Canute; p23, Norman
arch; and p29 Norman craftworkers: Mark Peppé

p32, Four Norman Kings:
Art Archive/British Library